WILD READS

Wolves

Karen Wallace

OXFORD
UNIVERSITY PRESS

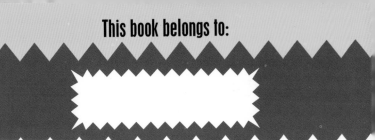

This book belongs to:

OXFORD
UNIVERSITY PRESS

Great Clarendon Street, Oxford OX2 6DP
Oxford University Press is a department of the University of Oxford.
It furthers the University's objective of excellence in research, scholarship,
and education by publishing worldwide in

Oxford   New York

Auckland   Cape Town   Dar es Salaam   Hong Kong   Karachi
Kuala Lumpur   Madrid   Melbourne   Mexico City   Nairobi
New Delhi   Shanghai   Taipei   Toronto

With offices in

Argentina   Austria   Brazil   Chile   Czech Republic   France   Greece
Guatemala   Hungary   Italy   Japan   Poland   Portugal   Singapore
South Korea   Switzerland   Thailand   Turkey   Ukraine   Vietnam

Oxford is a registered trade mark of Oxford University Press
in the UK and in certain other countries

Text © Karen Wallace
Illustrations © Jonathan Pointer
The moral rights of the author have been asserted

Database right Oxford University Press (maker)

This edition 2009

British Library Cataloguing in Publication Data

Data available

ISBN: 978-0-19-911935-6

1 3 5 7 9 10 8 6 4 2

Printed in China
Paper used in the production of this book is a natural,
recyclable product made from wood grown in sustainable forests.
The manufacturing process conforms to the environmental
regulations of the country of origin.

Contents

▶ Wolf hunting grounds

Deep in a forest
a grey wolf is howling.

High on a mountain
a brown wolf is hunting.

Across a wasteland
a white wolf is running.

Wolves roam and hunt in
wild places where there are no people.

grey wolf

brown wolf

white wolf

Did you know...

Two hundred years ago there were many thousands of wolves. Now there are only a few thousand left because most of their homelands have been destroyed.

▶ The grey wolf

A wolf is resting in a meadow. His fur is grey and his eyes are yellow. When he stands, he's huge and heavy. He weighs as much as a grown-up man.

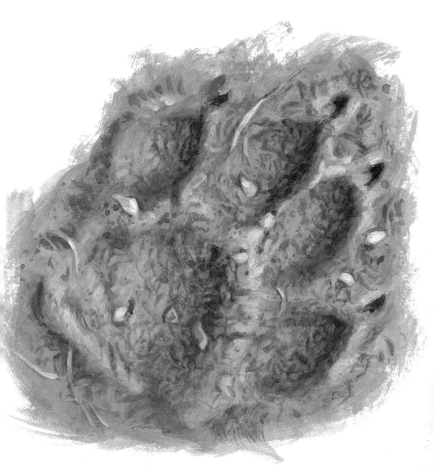

front footprint

When he walks,
his paws leave
print marks.
They're almost
as big as a
man's hand!

Did you know...
A wolf's front
footprint is bigger
than his back
footprint.

▶ Wolf pack

Six more wolves come into the meadow. They all belong to the grey wolf's pack.

A wolf pack is a family and the grey wolf leads them.

The grey wolf decides where the wolf pack hunts. The grey wolf decides when the wolf pack rests.

The grey wolf chooses a brown wolf for his mate. Only she will be a mother and have his cubs.

Did you know...
The size of a wolf pack depends on how much food it can find.

▶ Wolf cubs

In springtime, when the days are warmer, the brown wolf finds a cave and has four cubs.

They're blind and deaf and look like puppies. They suck her milk and start to grow.

A few weeks later, when the cubs have teeth, their mother chews up meat and feeds it to them.

Did you know...
Wolf cubs are born with blue eyes.
They turn to yellow when they are three months old.

Wolf cubs tumble in the sunshine.
They pretend to fight.
They pretend to hunt.
They watch and learn from the wolves around them.

Did you know...
The whole wolf pack helps to look after the cubs.

▶ Wolf voices

A wolf pack howls for many reasons.

One howl is thin and high and lonely. That wolf is calling for a mate.

One howl is fierce. It's a warning for other wolves to keep away.

One howl is deep and strong and joyful. This grey wolf has food to feed his pack.

Did you know...
Wolves also howl to show they are happy when cubs are born.

Wolf signals

Wolf packs have rules they all obey.

When there's food, the grey wolf eats first. If a young wolf is hungry and crawls too near, the grey wolf shows his teeth and growls a warning.

When the young wolf whimpers and rolls on to his back, that means he's sorry and he'll wait his turn.

Wolves say different things with their faces and bodies.

I am happy.

I am angry.

I am ready.

▶ Wolf senses

The grey wolf is sitting in the meadow.

With his ears, he hears a mole in the ground.

With his nose, he smells a deer
in the grass.

With his eyes, he sees a fly on
a flower.

The grey wolf uses all his senses.
He needs each one to stay alive.

Did you know...
Wolves have extraordinary
memories. They never forget what they
have seen, heard or smelt.

► Wolf food

The wolf pack gathers in the meadow. They're hungry. Food is hard to find.

Their favourite food is deer and caribou, but they've only eaten mice and weasels.

The grey wolf stops. He sniffs and listens. A moose is hiding in the forest.

snails

worms

mice

fish

weasels

rabbit

hares

deer

moose

Did you know…
A wolf can live
without food for
two weeks or more.

23

▶ Wolf hunt

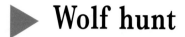

The grey wolf runs and the others follow.

A wolf pack always hunts together.

They run in line behind their leader. Their long, strong legs pound through the snow. If the leader gets tired, a new wolf takes over.

The pack chases the moose until he falls.

The wolves attack and their razor-sharp teeth tear up the meat.

Did you know...
A wolf's jaw is powerful enough to break a moose's leg bone.

Wild wolf

The wolf pack is resting in the meadow.

They've eaten the moose and their stomachs are full.

Suddenly the grey wolf senses danger.
He sniffs the air and looks around him.
His yellow eyes are wild and wary.

The wolf gets up and the others follow.

The grey wolf leads them deep into the forest.

They run to a place where no one will find them.

Glossary

 caribou A caribou is a large deer-like animal. **22**

 cub A young wolf is called a cub. **12, 13, 15, 17**

 howl A howl is a long, loud, crying noise. **4, 16, 17**

 hunt To hunt means to chase and kill other animals for food. **4, 10, 15, 24**

 mate A mate is one of a pair of animals that come together to have young. **10, 16**

 moose A moose is a large animal with antlers. **22, 26, 27**

pack A pack is a group of animals that live as one family.

8, 10, 11, 15-18, 22, 24, 26, 27

 roam To roam means to wander about.

4

 senses Using our senses means being able to see, smell, hear, touch and taste things.

20, 21

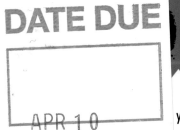

READS

your child develop a love of reading and
our world. See the websites and places
to visit below to learn more about wolves.

Wolves

WEBSITES
http://www.bbc.co.uk/cbbc/wild/amazinganimals/

http://kids.nationalgeographic.com/

http://www.wolf.org/wolves/index.asp

PLACES TO VISIT
The Highland Wildlife Park
http://www.highlandwildlifepark.org/index.html

UK Wolf Conservation Trust
http://www.ukwolf.org/
Take a walk on the wild side!

The Cotswold Wildlife Park
http://www.cotswoldwildlifepark.co.uk/